In the thirty years I've been serving kids and families, at no time have I seen parents more excited and committed to training their children and being involved in their lives than today. Today's parents are just looking for the right tools. David and Naomi Shibley's *Special Times With God* is one of those "right tools." This book is a wonderful way busy parents can jump-start a new day or conclude one in a special way at bedtime. These practical and important truths are a must-know for today's kids! Thanks, David and Naomi, for providing such a vital tool to help the family. It's a joy to recommend this book to you, the reader!

—JIM WIDEMAN
Children's and Family Ministry
Specialist and Consultant
www.jimwideman.com

Never have I known a time when family devotions were more important than the day we are living in. It's never too soon or too late to start, and *Special Times With God* provides everything you need to do it well. This is an area where we cannot drop the ball. Let's step up to the plate for our children and grandchildren.

—TERRY MEEUWSEN
Co-host, *The 700 Club*

Now that my children are grown and faithfully serving God as adults in the local church, I can look back with much better parental perspective and see how "special" David and Naomi Shibley's book *Special Times With God* really is! I believe the release of this edition will have a multiplied and transforming impact on future generations.

—PASTOR SAM WALKER
Church on the Rock North
Beaumont, Texas

Dr. David and Naomi Shibley bring a wealth of wisdom to the simple, yet powerful practice of family devotions. In this fast-paced, media-soaked culture parents need all the help they can get in order to fully focus in on their role as the primary teachers and pastors of their children. *Special Times With God* is perfect for moms and dads who are looking for tools to assist them in planting the Word of God into the hearts and lives of their children… it is a gift for young families like mine!

—PHIL JOEL
Recording artist and founder of deliberatePeople and deliberateKids

Dr. David and Naomi Shibley have been incredible mentors and friends over the years. Their wisdom and insight was priceless as we were raising our own small children! This book is full of time-tested thoughts that not only bring the family closer, but also most importantly build a strong foundation of biblical truth in the lives of children.

In a world full of half-truths and mixed messages being broadcast to children from the time they are born, it is vital for parents to teach their children to have a strong faith in God at an early age. Every family that uses this devotional will be blessed as they spend time learning together who God is.

—RON LUCE
President and Founder of Teen Mania Ministries

We are happy to recommend *Special Times With God* as a devotional book that will greatly aid parents in that all-important privilege of devotional times with their children. As children's workers as well as grandparents ourselves, we see an increasing need for families to pray, worship and learn together. This book is an excellent tool to help parents guide their children into the truths of the Kingdom of God.

—DANNY AND PEGGY THORNTON
Missionaries and Trainers of Children's Teachers
Beyond Ourselves Ministries

SPECIAL TIMES WITH

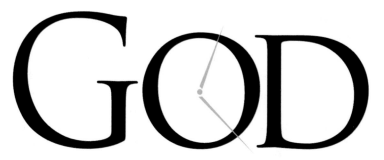

GOD

FAMILY DEVOTIONS WITH
YOUNG CHILDREN

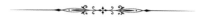

DAVID & NAOMI SHIBLEY

SPECIAL TIMES WITH GOD by David and Naomi Shibley
Published by Creation House
A Strang Company
600 Rinehart Road
Lake Mary, Florida 32746
www.creationhouse.com

Cover design by Marvin Eans
Interior design by Terry Clifton

Library of Congress Control Number: 2007931863
International Standard Book Number: 978-1-59979-223-1
First Edition
08 09 10 11 — 987654321
Printed in the United States of America

To Our Sons,

Their Families,

and

All the Children of the World.

"Jesus loves the little children,

All the children of the world."

A WORD TO PARENTS

This book grew out of our own needs as new parents. When our sons were young, there were several excellent family devotional materials available. However, we were searching for a book that combined Scripture memorization, a brief story, a simple catechism, an aid to family discussion, and an aid to prayer, all while reinforcing the basic truth of the gospel. This book is the result of that search.

We studied to find a system for family devotions that was both workable and flexible. Through our frustrations, failures, and victories, we arrived at some principles that we're convinced are valid.

1. *Brevity is the key.* When it comes to communicating the faith to young children, multiple short dosages are usually best. Our own attention span is sometimes short; how much more our children's! So we have worked to keep each session no longer than five minutes. We know now that the strength of family devotions lies not in length but in consistency.

2. *Repetition is vital to learning.* The book is divided into seven sections, each section containing several sessions. Each session is designed to be read and reinforced for a week. One major truth is presented each week.

The repetition of a specific truth at spaced intervals yields exciting results. God commanded the parents of Israel to reinforce His truth to their children at four natural points during the day: "And these words which I command you today shall be in your heart; you shall teach them diligently to your children, and shall talk of them when you sit in your house, when you walk by the way, when you lie down, and when you rise up" (Deut. 6:6–7).

Today we don't "walk by the way," we drive—to school, soccer practice, or other activities. Families today are very busy, but with discipline you can still "sit in your house" together at mealtimes. That is why we've kept these devotions short. The verses and key truths can be reinforced in the daily routines of eating together, driving together, beginning the day, and ending the day.

3. *Children should be taught essential truths of Scripture.* The first section is devoted to that theme that all spiritual growth is predicated on one's understanding of the character of God. Obviously the character of God is a vast subject. Parents should feel free to interject their own insights and experiences throughout this

section and the entire book. Perhaps no one can be more successful in relating concepts to children than their own parents.

For example, in the session "God Made You," parents may wish to share with the child how they prepared for him or her even before birth. Share with your child how you prayed for him and how God lovingly answered your prayers. In short, these sessions are not meant to be purely didactic. They are meant to be an opportunity for you to impart your faith to your child.

We are strong proponents of child evangelism, since both of us came to faith in Christ at early ages. We're convinced it is never too early to share the gospel with children. A recent study indicated that children were more familiar with Ronald McDonald than with Jesus. America's children suffer not from overexposure to Jesus but from underexposure to Him, so this book is unapologetically evangelistic in tone. Jesus said, "Let the little children come to me, and do not forbid them; for of such is the kingdom of God" (Mark 10:14).

In a culture that has cut itself loose from its Judeo-Christian moorings and is consequently drowning in the muck of subjectivism, the Ten Commandments provide our children the stability and direction they need and deserve. Likewise, the Beatitudes form a basis for a genuinely Christian system of ethics and behavior.

Right living stems from right thinking. Consequently the content of these devotions is strong in basic Christian doctrine. The Apostles' Creed, a very early baptismal confession, is one of the most universal of all the church's statements. It is a clear summary of Christian belief and a deposit of truth to be planted in fertile young minds and hearts.

4. *Scripture memory is crucial.* King David said, "Your word I have hidden in my heart, that I might not sin against You" (Ps. 119:11).

We are grateful for the many translations of Scripture available today. We encourage you to use the translation of your preference when memorizing verses with your children. Because we grew up with the King James Version of the Bible, the New King James Version provided continuity and familiarity in transmitting Scripture from our generation to our sons. Since this book was first written for our own family devotions, we have retained the New King James Version. Far more important than which translation is chosen is the imperative of getting God's Word into our children's minds and hearts.

5. *Life must be imparted!* Books can't do that. They provide information, but that's not enough. Only Jesus Christ can give spiritual life. Our children will see Him,

or fail to see Him, as they observe our lives. We must be ever mindful that the goal of all our instruction is to see our children experience a vibrant, living relationship with Jesus Christ as their Savior and Lord.

When *Special Times With God* was first published, our two sons were little boys. Now they are grown, married, and serving Jesus Christ. We have added two beautiful Christian daughters-in-law to our family, and now we are grandparents. We're still learning how to have more effective family devotions. When we began using the contents of this book in our family time, the results were so encouraging that we had to share them. We've known firsthand the mixture of duty and despair that so many Christian parents feel regarding family devotions. We're grateful for the overwhelming response this book has received through the years. Now we pray it will bring blessing to you, your children, and grandchildren.

The practice of family devotions yields strong, lasting results. This small investment will yield valuable, even eternal dividends. May God use this book to bring blessings to you and your family for years to come.

—DAVID AND NAOMI SHIBLEY

CONTENTS

IV. GOD'S SPIRIT MAKES US LIKE JESUS

V. HOW TO MAKE GOD HAPPY

VI. JESUS TAUGHT US HOW TO LIVE

VII. SOME VERY IMPORTANT WORDS

APPENDIX

FOREWORD

Christian parents today are faced with one of the greatest challenges and responsibilities ever undertaken: the godly upbringing of their children. In a culture where Christian values and parental authority are being attacked and undermined on every front, parents cannot take their task too seriously or begin spiritual training too early. Be assured that the principalities and powers of spiritual darkness against which Christian parents must battle are determined to destroy our children from the time they are born.

This book is for parents who have understood and accepted their duty—indeed, their privilege—of teaching their children about God and His ways and of leading them into a personal relationship with the Lord Jesus Christ. It is designed for young families who want to begin a tradition of family devotions that are meaningful and fundamental to Christian growth and character. The fifty-eight sessions, which can be covered in a year's time (with extras for special occasions and holidays), lay a solid foundation for a child's future spiritual understanding.

I heartily commend this book to you, and I personally thank David and Naomi Shibley for this valuable contribution to the preservation of Christian family life.

—TIM LaHAYE

I

WHAT GOD IS LIKE

GOD MADE THE WORLD

Let's Remember

In the beginning God created the heavens and the earth.

—GENESIS 1:1

Let's Listen

Look up! God made the sun, moon, stars, and sky. Look around! God made the trees, plants, and animals. He made pretty flowers. He made food in our gardens. He made the oceans and rivers and fish of the sea. God made people too. He created the world. That means He made everything out of nothing.

Everything God made is for His glory. That means that everything everywhere was made to please God.

Let's Answer

Question: Who made everything?

Answer: God made everything.

Name some things God made.

> *Thank you, God, for making everything beautiful.*
> *Help me take good care of Your world. Amen.**

---

* These are guides to prayer. Parents should encourage their children in spontaneous expressions of prayer and praise to God.

5

GOD MADE YOU

I will praise You, for I am fearfully and wonderfully made.

—Psalm 139:14

After God made the world, He made a man named Adam and a woman named Eve. All the people of the world came from them.

There is nobody else just like you. God made you special, and He has something important for you to do.

God made people so they could love Him. We call this being made in God's image. This makes people more important than anything else God made.

Question: Who made you?

Answer: God made me.

Question: Why are people so important?

Answer: Because people are made in God's image.

You can see your image in a mirror. Who is reflected in the mirror? What do you think it means to be made in God's image?

Thank You, God, for making me. Thank You for my body. Thank You for my mind. Thank You that I can know You. I'm glad You have given me something important to do with my life. Help me to live my life for You. Amen.

Our Great God

> Go therefore and make disciples of all the nations,
> baptizing them in the name of the Father and of
> the Son and of the Holy Spirit.
>
> —Matthew 28:19

Let's Listen

There is one God who exists forever. He has always
been. He always will be.

God the Father loves all the people of the world very
much, so He sent His Son, Jesus, from heaven to earth
to be born as a baby. He died to save us from our sins.
The Holy Spirit guides the church and lives inside all
true Christians.

God is a trinity. *Trinity* means "three in one." God
the Father, God the Son, and God the Holy Spirit are
present with you every day.*

8

Let's Answer

Question: What does *trinity* mean?

Answer: Trinity means "three in one."

Question: What three Persons make up the one true God?

Answer: God the Father, God the Son, and God the Holy Spirit.

Let's Talk About It

What are some things Jesus did to show us what His Father is like? How can the Holy Spirit guide you?

Let's Pray Together

Dear God, You are the one true God. I love You, Father. I love You, Jesus. I love You, Holy Spirit. Amen.

---

* Parents may want to use the analogy of water, ice, and steam to help older children understand the concept of three in one. This can be done by putting ice cubes beside a cup of steaming hot water and explaining that water exists in three ways: solid, liquid, and gas. Likewise, God is three persons: the Father, the Son, and the Holy Spirit.

GOD IS LOVE

God is love.

—1 JOHN 4:8

God the Father loves everyone in the world. He loves you. You are very special to Him. The Father loves you so much that He sent His Son, Jesus, from heaven. God gave His Son to die for you. That's how you can know He loves you. The Bible says, "But God demonstrates His own love toward us, in that while we were still sinners, Christ died for us" (Rom. 5:8).

How do you feel toward a person who makes fun of you or hits you? It's hard to love someone like that, isn't it? But God loves us even when we don't love and obey Him. It is a sin not to love and obey God, and God must punish sin. That's why He sent Jesus to take the punishment for us, because all of us have sinned. You see, God loves us so much He was willing to be punished in our place. That would be like your asking to be spanked in place of your brother or sister who did something wrong. See how much God loves you?

Let's Answer

Question: How do you know God the Father loves you?

Answer: He sent Jesus to die for me.

Let's Talk About It

Some people think God doesn't love them. How do we know He does love them?

Let's Pray Together

Thank You, God, for loving me. Thank You for sending Jesus to die for me. This shows me how much You love me. Amen.

11

GOD IS HOLY

Let's Remember

But as He who has called you is holy, you also be holy in all your conduct.

—1 PETER 1:15

Let's Listen

God is holy. He is like no one else. That's because He thinks and does only what is right. God wants us to be holy too. That means He wants us to belong to Him and to love and obey him. Instead of thinking bad thoughts, He wants us to think good thoughts. Instead of doing wrong things, He wants us to do what is right and good. God can help us do the right things. God is happy when we ask Him to make us holy, and we are happy too.

Let's Answer

Question: What does it mean to be holy?

Answer: To be holy means to belong to God and to love and obey Him.

God has never done anything wrong. This is because He is holy. He wants to make us holy too. When are some times you need God to help you be holy? For example, what should you do if someone says mean things about you?

Let's Pray Together

Thank You, God, for being holy. I'm glad that You think and do only what is right. Help me to live like that too. Amen.

GOD IS OUR FATHER

But as many as received [Jesus], to them He gave
the right to become children of God.

—JOHN 1:12

God created everyone, but not every person has God
for his heavenly Father. When someone invites Jesus
into his life, God becomes his Father in heaven. Most
of us have fathers living here with us on earth. How
wonderful that we can have God as our Father too! He
loves us even more than our father on earth loves us.
He always is able to give us what we need. He will take
care of us perfectly.

Question: When does God become your Father?

Answer: When I receive Jesus into my life.

What are some ways God is a good Father to us?

Jesus taught us to pray in this way:

> Our Father in heaven,
> Hallowed be Your name.
> Your Kingdom come.
> Your will be done.
> On earth as it is in heaven.
> Give us this day our daily bread.
> And forgive us our debts,
> As we forgive our debtors.
> And do not lead us into temptation,
> But deliver us from the evil one.
> For Yours is the kingdom
>   and the power
>   and the glory forever. Amen.
>   —MATTHEW 6:9–13

God's Son Is Jesus

> Simon Peter answered and said, "You are the Christ, the Son of the living God."
>
> —Matthew 16:16

Let's Listen

Jesus is God and He is also a man (Matt. 1:23, Rom. 5:17). This is difficult to understand, and even adults can't explain it. They can only say that the Bible teaches it. The Bible calls this a mystery.

God arranged to have Jesus be born just like any other baby. He grew up like us. Since Jesus is a man, He was sometimes tired and hungry. But since Jesus is God, He never did one thing that was sinful or wrong. Jesus is God's special-born Son who lived forever with His Father in heaven before coming to Earth. The Bible calls Him God's "only begotten Son" (John 3:16). Jesus is today God and man all at once.

Question: Who is God's special-born Son?

Answer: Jesus is God's special-born Son.

Name some ways that Jesus is special and like no one else.

Thank You, Jesus, for showing me what Your Father is like. I know God the Father loves me because You love me, and You are God and Man both at once. I believe that You were special-born from heaven, that You were born on Earth, and are the Son of the living God. Amen.

God's Spirit Is in Our World

Let's Remember

> When He, the Spirit of truth has come, He will
> guide you into all truth.
>
> —John 16:13

Let's Listen

We call God's Spirit the Holy Spirit. The Holy Spirit lets someone know he needs Jesus in his life. After a person becomes a follower of Jesus, the Holy Spirit comes and lives inside and makes him able to be the kind of person that makes God happy. The Bible calls these good things "the fruit of the Spirit" (Gal. 5:22-23). The Holy Spirit gives special gifts to Christians. He also helps them live like Jesus.

Let's Answer

Question: Who makes people know they need Jesus in their lives?

Answer: The Holy Spirit.

Question: Who makes Christians able to live a life that pleases God?

Answer: The Holy Spirit.

Let's Talk About It

What do you need the Holy Spirit to help you do?

Let's Pray Together

Holy Spirit, You are God, just as Jesus is God and the heavenly Father is God. Help me to know when You speak to me, and help me to obey You always. Amen.

II

GOD GAVE RULES FOR
A GOOD LIFE

You Shall Have No Other Gods Before Me

Let's Remember

> You shall have no other gods before Me.
>
> —Exodus 20:3

Let's Listen

God gave rules to Moses for the people of Israel to obey. We call these rules the Ten Commandments. When we obey God's commands, we make God happy.

The first rule commands us to worship and serve God alone. No person or thing should take the first place in our lives, which only God deserves. We must never let anyone or anything be more important to us than God.

Let's Answer

Question: Who should be most important in your life?

Answer: God should be most important in my life.

What are some things that could become more important to us than God, if we let them?

Dear God, I will worship and serve You alone. May nothing ever be more important to me than You. Amen.

YOU SHALL NOT MAKE ANY GRAVEN IMAGE

You shall not make for yourself any graven image.

—EXODUS 20:4

Some people don't worship the true and living God. They worship gods they make themselves—statues of wood, stone, or metal. These statues are not the real God. They cannot hear or answer when people pray to them. They are false gods. The Bible calls them "graven images" or "idols."

But an idol can be *anything* that becomes more important to us than God. We must not have any idols in our lives.

Questions: What is an idol?

Answer: An idol is anything that is more important to me than God.

What are some things that could become idols in your life?

Dear God, You are the true and living God. May I never have any idol in my life. I will love and serve You with my whole heart. Amen.

You Shall Not Take the Name of the Lord Your God in Vain

> You shall not take the name of the Lord your God in vain.
>
> —Exodus 20:7

When people use God's name without proper respect, they are taking His name in vain. People sometimes curse, using the name of God the Father or Jesus, His Son. God clearly commands us not to do this. God promises that those who take His name in vain will one day answer to Him for it.

When we speak God's name we must always remember that He is the almighty God, the ruler of heaven and earth. His name is always to be spoken with respect.

Questions: What does it mean to take God's name in vain?

Answer: When people speak God's name without proper respect, they are taking His name in vain.

How can we make sure we will never take God's name in vain?

Help me, God, to be very careful what I say. May I always respect and honor You and Your name in all that I say and do. Amen.

Remember the Sabbath Day to Keep It Holy

Let's Remember

Remember the Sabbath day, to keep it holy.

—Exodus 20:8

Let's Listen

God rested on the seventh day after He had created the heavens, earth, and man. He has told us, too, to take one day of rest each week.

Most Christians worship together on Sundays to celebrate that Jesus rose from the dead on the first day of the week. This is our special day for the Lord, and it should be a day set aside for God. On that day we should worship God, remember all the wonderful things He has done, and rest with our family.

Let's Answer

Question: How can you keep Sunday holy?

Answer: By worshiping God, remembering all the wonderful things He has done, and resting with my family.

What should our family do to keep the sabbath day holy?

Dear God, help me to remember to make Sunday a special day just for You. Amen.

Honor Your Father and Your Mother

> Honor your father and your mother, that your days
> may be long upon the land.
>
> —Exodus 20:12

God gave us parents because He loves us. God uses parents to bring us into His world and to protect us and to help us love and obey God.

We honor our parents by obeying them. We should always be respectful of them and do what they say. We should try to please our parents by doing what we know is right. This pleases God too. God promises a long life to those who honor their parents.

Question: How do you honor your parents?

Answer: I honor my parents by obeying them and respecting them.

What are some ways that you could show that you honor your parents?

Thank You, God, for my parents. Help me to always respect them and obey them. Amen.

You Shall Not Murder

You shall not murder.

—Exodus 20:13

Every person is very special to God. Even before we were born, God knew about us, cared about us, and loved us. Since God has given us life, we should never plan to take life away, ours or anyone else's.

We are to respect our own lives and the lives of others. God gave every person the great gift of life. We are to protect this wonderful gift.

Question: Who gave you life?

Answer: God gave me life.

Questions: How should you treat this gift of life?

Answer: I should thank God for life, respect life, and protect life.

What are some ways you can show respect for your own life and for the lives of others?

> *Thank You, God, for my life and for the lives of others. May I always respect and protect the lives of all people. Amen.*

You Shall Not Commit Adultery

Let's Remember

You shall not commit adultery.

—Exodus 20:14

Let's Listen

God loves families very much. He gave rules to keep families happy. Adultery is when a husband or wife lives with someone other than the person he or she married. This makes many people sad. God says, "Don't!"

How happy we are when we obey God's rules! God is happy with us, and we are happy with ourselves.

Let's Answer

Question: Why should people never commit adultery?

Answer: Because God commands us not to commit adultery. He knows it makes many people sad.

When you grow up, God may want you to get married. If He does, He will want you to love and live with the person you marry for the rest of your life. That means loving that person even when he or she is mean or selfish. Who loves us that way? How can we learn to love others no matter what they do or say to us?

Let's Pray

> *Dear God, I pray that You will keep me pure in my thoughts and in my body. If You want me to marry one day, give me a happy Christian home where we all can love and serve You. Amen.*

You Shall Not Steal

You shall not steal.

—Exodus 20:15

Let's Listen

Stealing is taking something that belongs to someone else. When someone takes something that isn't his, God sees it and He is not pleased.

Stealing is against God's law. It is sin. It is also against the laws of our country, so never take things that don't belong to you.

Let's Answer

Question: What is stealing?

Answer: Stealing is taking something that belongs to someone else.

Why is it wrong to steal? What can happen to people who steal?

> *Dear God, help me always to be careful with what belongs to others. May I never take anything that isn't mine. Amen.*

You Shall Not Bear False Witness

Let's Remember

You shall not bear false witness.

—Exodus 20:16

Let's Listen

"Bearing false witness" means saying something that isn't true. It is lying. God commands us not to lie. Telling the truth is very important to God.

Sometimes people lie to get others in trouble. Sometimes people lie because they are afraid to tell the truth. It is never right to lie for any reason. God always wants us to tell the truth.

Let's Answer

Question: What does it mean to bear false witness?

Answer: To bear false witness means to say something that isn't true.

Sometimes it seems that it would be easier to lie than to tell the truth. When are some of those times? Remember that even in those times we should tell the truth. It's always better to tell the truth. Why is that true?

Let's Pray

Dear God, help me to always tell the truth, even if I want to lie. Amen.

YOU SHALL NOT COVET

You shall not covet.

—Exodus 20:17

"Boy, I wish I could have *his* toys!"

Have you ever heard anyone say that? That's an example of what the Bible calls coveting. Coveting is wanting something that belongs to someone else. Coveting often leads to stealing. Instead of coveting, we should thank God for what we already have. We should be glad other people have what they have.

Question: What is coveting?

Answer: Coveting is to want something that belongs to someone else.

Name some things people sometimes covet.

> *Thank You, God, for everything You have given me. Help me not to wish for anything that belongs to someone else. Amen.*

III

WHY JESUS CAME TO EARTH

Sin and God's Love

> For all have sinned and fall short of the glory of God.
>
> —Romans 3:23

Let's Listen

Adam and Eve disobeyed God in the Garden of Eden. People have been disobeying God ever since then. When we do not obey God, we are sinning. Sometimes we sin by what we think. Sometimes we sin by what we do.

God hates sin. It causes people to live away from God, and people die because of sin. He must punish our sin.

But God did not want us to be separated from Him. He sent His own Son, Jesus, to take the punishment that we deserved. Our sins are forgiven when we turn from them and ask Jesus into our lives. Just think how much God loves us!

Questions: What is sin?

Answer: Sin is not obeying God.

Question: Has everybody sinned?

Answer: Yes. Romans 3:23 says, "*All* have sinned..."

Let's Talk About It

What are some ways that people don't obey God?

Let's Pray Together

Thank You, God, for loving me even though I have sinned. Thank You for sending Jesus to take the punishment for my sins. Amen.

BABY JESUS

> For God so loved the world He gave His only begotten Son, that whoever believes in Him should not perish but have everlasting life.
>
> —JOHN 3:16

God looked down on the earth and saw all the people disobeying Him, but He still loved them! God the Father loves all people. He doesn't want anyone to die and be away from Him forever.

God sent Jesus, His wonderful, eternal Son, to pay for our sins. He came to Earth as a little baby. Jesus was born in the little town of Bethlehem. He was born in a manger where animals lived. That was the world's most wonderful night!

God was His Father, and Mary was Jesus' mother. Jesus was God's special-born Son, who was born to Mary on Earth.

God chose Joseph, Mary's husband, to help care for Jesus when He was a child. An angel told Joseph, "You shall call His name Jesus, for He will save His people from their sins" (Matt. 1:21).

Let's Answer

Question: Why did God send Jesus to Earth?

Answer: Because He loved us enough to send His Son to pay for our sins.

Let's Talk About It

What made Jesus such a special baby?

Let's Pray Together

Thank You, Jesus, for coming all the way from heaven. Thank You for being born as a little baby. I'm glad you know what it's like to be my age too. Amen.

JESUS GREW TOO!

And Jesus increased in wisdom and stature, and in favor with God and men.

—LUKE 2:52

When Jesus was a child, He grew just as you are growing. He became wiser as He grew older. His body got bigger and stronger. Jesus loved His Father in heaven and other people, and God was very pleased with Jesus too.

Jesus enjoyed being with other children. He also liked to go with Mary and Joseph to the temple to worship God, His Father.

Because Jesus grew just as you are growing, He knows what it is like to be your age. You can always talk to Jesus, and He will always understand.

Question: How did Jesus grow as a child?

Answer: Jesus grew in His mind and in His body. He also grew in favor with God and people.

Let's Talk About It

Does Jesus understand what it's like to be your age? Why?

Let's Pray Together

> *Thank You, Jesus, that You know what it's like to be my age. Help me to grow as You did. Amen.*

Jesus Did
Wonderful Things

Let's Remember

> How God anointed Jesus of Nazareth with the
> Holy Spirit and with power, who went about doing
> good and healing all who were oppressed by the
> devil, for God was with Him.
>
> —Acts 10:38

Let's Listen

Jesus did many wonderful things. The people loved to
listen to Him. He told them the good news that what
they had waited to see for so long was now here. God's
Son, their Savior, had come.

How exciting it was when Jesus came to town! Jesus
did many miracles. A miracle is something only God can
do. He made blind people to see and crippled people to
walk. Many people had been made sad and afraid by the
devil. Jesus took their fear away and made them happy

again. When Jesus touched people they were never the same again.

Let's Answer

Question: Jesus did many miracles. What is a miracle?

Answer: A miracle is something only God can do.

Let's Talk About It

Name some wonderful things Jesus did while He was here on earth. Name some wonderful things Jesus is still doing today.

Let's Pray Together

Thank You, Jesus, for caring about people. I'm glad that You care when we are hurt, sad, or afraid. I'm glad that You can change us and make us well, happy, and not afraid. Amen.

Jesus Died for You

Christ died for our sins according to the Scriptures,
and...He was buried, and...He rose again the third
day according to the Scriptures.

—1 Corinthians 15:3–4

Let's Listen

Jesus never did anything wrong. But when He grew up
some people didn't like what He was saying and doing,
so they made plans to kill Him. When they arrested
Jesus and brought Him to Pilate, the Roman ruler, he
said he did not believe Jesus had done anything wrong.
But when the people began to yell, "Crucify Him!"
Pilate allowed Jesus to be nailed to the cross.

First, the soldiers whipped Jesus' back. A crown of
large thorns was pressed onto His head. Then Jesus
carried His own cross as far as He could toward Mount
Calvary. There the soldiers put nails through His hands
and feet. The people spat on Him and laughed at Him,

but even then He loved them. He said, "Father, forgive them, for they do not know what they do" (Luke 23:34).

Just before He died, Jesus said, "It is finished" (John 19:30). He took the full punishment for all our sins on the cross. He died for all people everywhere, but He also died just for you.

Let's Answer

Question: What did Jesus mean when He said, "It is finished"?

Answer: Jesus meant that He had made the full payment for all our sins.

Let's Talk About It

It looked like the devil had won when Jesus died on the cross. But he didn't win. Jesus really won, and so did we. Why is that true?

Let's Pray Together

Dear Jesus, You love me much more than I could ever understand. Thank You for dying for me. Thank You for taking the punishment for my sins. Amen.

Jesus Is Alive!

Let's Remember

> I am He who lives, and was dead, and behold, I am
> alive forevermore.
>
> —Revelation 1:18

Let's Listen

Three days after Jesus died some women went to His tomb. They were amazed to see an angel there who said, "He is not here; for He is risen, as He said" (Matt. 28:6). The women ran to tell Jesus' followers, the disciples, this great news. At first, the disciples didn't believe them. But Peter and John ran to Jesus' tomb to see for themselves. It was true! He had risen, just as He had promised.

Jesus is still alive today. All power has been given to Him. He is the mighty ruler of heaven and Earth. Death and hell could not hold him. He broke free! Jesus said, "Because I live, you will live also" (John 14:19).

Question: Is Jesus alive today?

Answer: Yes! Jesus is alive today. (Recite Revelation 1:18.)

Because Jesus rose from the dead, what will happen to His followers when they die?

Dear Jesus,
I'm glad I don't
worship someone
who is dead and
cannot hear me. Many
people in the world pray
to false gods like that. I'm
thankful You are alive!
You really hear me when
I talk to You. Because
You live forever, I can live
forever too. Amen.

55

JESUS IS COMING BACK

> If I go and prepare a place for you, I will come again
> and receive you to Myself; that where I am, there
> you may be also.
>
> —JOHN 14:3

Jesus promised that one day He would come back to earth. When He returns, He won't come as a little baby. This time He will come as the mighty King of kings and Lord of lords. Wicked people will no longer be in control. There will be peace in all the world. Children won't be afraid anymore. Jesus will rule the earth with His great love.

When this happens, loud voices in heaven will say, "The kingdoms of this world have become the kingdoms of our Lord and of His Christ, and He shall reign forever and ever!" (Rev. 11:15). What a wonderful time that will be!

Question: Who will one day rule over the earth?

Answer: Jesus will one day rule over the earth.

What do you think it will be like when Jesus rules over the earth?

Thank You, Lord Jesus, that one day You will rule over the whole earth. I'm glad I know that one day You will make everything right. Amen.

JESUS IS THE ONLY WAY TO GOD

> Jesus said to him. "I am the way, the truth, and
> the life. No one comes to the Father except
> through Me."
>
> —JOHN 14:6

There are many religions in the world. They were started by men, not by God. Only Jesus is both God and man at once. Only Jesus died to take the punishment for our sins. Only Jesus rose from the dead. Only Jesus will one day return for all those who believe in Him and love Him.

Many sincere people try to reach God by some way other than Jesus. But Jesus said He is the only way to God. We cannot get to heaven unless we come God's way. The way to God is through His Son Jesus Christ. Jesus said, "I am the door. If anyone enters by Me, he will be saved" (John 10:9).

Since Jesus is the only way to heaven, the church sends missionaries all over the world to tell people this important truth. They tell people the good news that God sent His Son to die for them and to bring them to His kingdom. If they believe in Him, they will not die but live forever (John 3:16).

Let's Answer

Question: Who is the only way to God and heaven?

Answer: Jesus is the only way to God and heaven.

Let's Talk About It

Since Jesus is the only way to God and heaven, how should we feel about those who haven't heard the good news about Jesus? (Read Romans 1:14-16.)

Let's Pray Together

Thank You, Jesus, for opening the way to God for everyone who puts his trust in You. You are the way to God and to heaven. Amen.

JESUS IS LORD AND SAVIOR

Let's Remember

> That if you confess with your mouth the Lord Jesus
> and believe in your heart that God has raised Him
> from the dead, you will be saved. For "whoever calls
> upon the name of the Lord will be saved."
>
> —ROMANS 10:9, 13

Let's Listen

It's important to know *about* Jesus, but it's even more
important for you to know *Him*. You can know Jesus by
turning from your sins and inviting Him to rule your
life. The Bible calls this being saved or born again.*

You know that Jesus is God's special-born Son. You
know that He never sinned but that He took the pun-

---

* Note to Parents: This could be a very meaningful time where your child
experiences a spiritual new birth. Parents will need to be sensitive to their
child's readiness and to the Holy Spirit's leading as they begin this devotional session. The "Let's Talk About It" and "Let's Pray Together" sections
may need to be altered if the child has already received Christ or if he or
she appears not to understand the significance of this act. Parents should
avoid having the child simply recite the prayer without a sincere declaration
of faith in Christ.

ishment for your sins when He died on the cross. You know that one day He will come back. You know that Jesus is the only way to God and heaven.

Jesus will come into your life if you will ask Him. When you ask Him into your life, you become God's child and part of God's family. The Bible says, "But as many as received Him, to them He gave the right to become children of God, even to those who believe in His name" (John 1:12).

Let's Answer

Question: How can you know Jesus?

Answer: I can know Jesus by turning from my sins and inviting Him into my life.

Let's Talk About It

Jesus is waiting for you to invite Him into your life. The Bible says, "Behold, now is the accepted time; behold, now is the day of salvation" (2 Cor. 6:2). Will you turn from your sins and ask Jesus to rule your life right now?

You can invite Jesus to come into your life right now. You can say something like this:

> *Lord Jesus, thank You for dying for me. I'm sorry for my sins. I turn away from them now and I turn to You. I trust You and You alone to get to heaven. I take You now as my own Savior. I will follow You as my Lord for the rest of my life. Thank You for hearing my prayer, forgiving my sins, and coming into my life, just as You promised. Amen.*

If you prayed that prayer from your heart, welcome to God's wonderful family! You have received Jesus, and He has received you. Jesus said, "All that the Father gives Me will come to Me, and the one who comes to me I will by no means cast out" (John 6:37). Now you can get to know Jesus even better!

JESUS IS PRAYING FOR YOU

Therefore He is also able to save to the uttermost those who come to God by Him, seeing He ever lives to make intercession for them.

—HEBREWS 7:25

Let's Listen

Jesus stayed on the Earth for forty days after He rose from the dead. He told His disciples that He had to go back to heaven but that He and His Father would send the Holy Spirit to them in His place. The disciples were to go into all the world and tell everyone the wonderful news about what Jesus had done for them. Jesus told the disciples that they were to teach people everywhere all He had taught them. The Holy Spirit would help them with this task.

After Jesus told them these things, He was taken up into heaven. There He sat down at the right hand of God His Father. From that time until now, Jesus has been asking God the Father to bless all those who have believed in Him. Just think: if you belong to Jesus He is talking to God about you!

Let's Answer

Question: What is Jesus doing in heaven?

Answer: Jesus is praying for those who believe in Him.

Let's Talk About It

It's so good to know that Jesus is on our side, defending us and praying for us. What are some things that you think Jesus talks to God the Father about?

Let's Pray Together

Dear Jesus, I'm glad that You keep on caring about us. You cared for people while You were on the Earth. But You still care for us now that You are in heaven. I'm glad You talk to God about all of those who believe in You. Amen.

Jesus, the Good Shepherd

> I will both lie down in peace, and sleep; for You alone, O Lord, make me dwell in safety.
>
> —Psalm 4:8

Sometimes people with sin in their lives do mean things to hurt other people. The Lord Jesus is able to protect you from every evil. That means He is able to keep you safe. You don't have to be afraid of anything, because He is strong enough to protect you.

The shepherd boy David knew the Lord would protect him. He wrote:

> The Lord is my shepherd; I shall not want. He makes me to lie down in green pastures; He leads me beside the still waters. He restores my soul; He leads me in the paths of righteousness For His name's sake. Yea, though I walk through the valley of the shadow of death, I will fear no evil; For You

are with me; Your rod and Your staff, they comfort me. You prepare a table before me in the presence of my enemies; You anoint my head with oil; My cup runs over. Surely goodness and mercy shall follow me All the days of my life; And I will dwell in the house of the Lord Forever.

—PSALM 23

Let's Answer

Question: Why don't you need to be afraid?

Answer: Because God is able to protect me.

Let's Talk About It

What are some things you've been afraid of? Why don't you need to be afraid of them anymore?

Let's Pray Together

Thank You, Lord Jesus, that You will keep me safe. I'm so glad that You are always with me. Now I don't have to be afraid. Amen.

IV

God's Spirit Makes
Us Like Jesus

GOD'S SPIRIT BRINGS LOVE

Let's Remember

The fruit of the Spirit is love.

—GALATIANS 5:22

Let's Listen

When a person invites Jesus into his life, the Holy Spirit begins to change him. God's Spirit begins to work inside the new Christian so he will think and act like Jesus.

When we let Jesus change us, we begin to love people more. Jesus takes hate and envy away. In its place, He gives us His love. Jesus said, "By this all will know that you are My disciples, if you have love for one another" (John 13:35).

Let's Answer

Question: How will people know if you are a follower of Jesus?

Answer: People will know I am a follower of Jesus by my love for all people.

Jesus gives His people love for other people. Who are some people you want Jesus to give you love for?

Thank You, Father, for sending the Holy Spirit to make me think and act like Jesus. I want You to change me so I can love people as You do. Amen.

71

God's Spirit Brings Joy

Let's Remember

The fruit of the Spirit is love, joy.

—GALATIANS 5:22

Let's Listen

Followers of Jesus have problems just like anyone else. But Christians have Jesus as their constant friend. He goes through the problems with us. The Holy Spirit gives us joy even when we're in trouble.

Of course, there are times when we are sad. Even in sad times we can have joy. We know that when things go wrong for us God causes everything to work out in a good way in the end. (Read Romans 8:28.)

Let's Answer

Question: Do Christians have problems?

Answer: Yes.

Question: Why can Christians have joy even when things go wrong?

Answer: Because God will work everything out in a good way in the end.

Let's Talk About It

What are some problems or troubles you have? Even when you have problems, how can you have the joy of the Lord?

Let's Pray Together

Thank You, Lord Jesus, that even in times of trouble I can have Your joy in my heart. It brings me joy just to think that I know You. I love You. Amen.

God's Spirit Brings Peace

The fruit of the Spirit is love, joy, peace.

—Galatians 5:22

Most people want their lives to be peaceful. Peace means not fighting or arguing with other people, and it means not being afraid of or angry with God. People fight with each other because they are fighting inside themselves. People who don't know God don't have peace inside. When we come to God by inviting Jesus into our lives, we have peace with God. As we obey the Lord, the peace of God takes the place of our fears and makes us feel safe.

Jesus promised His followers, "Peace I leave with you, My peace I give to you; not as the world gives do I give to you. Let not your heart be troubled, neither let it be afraid" (John 14:27).

Question: What does *peace* mean?

Answer: It means not fighting or arguing with others and not being afraid or angry with God or any person.

Question: Why do people fight with each other?

Answer: Because people are fighting within themselves.

Question: How do we make peace with God?

Answer: We make peace with God by inviting Jesus into our lives.

What kind of peace does Jesus give us?

Thank You, Lord Jesus, for giving me peace inside. Because I know You, I have peace with You. Because I am at peace with You and with myself, I can be at peace with others. Amen.

GOD'S SPIRIT BRINGS LONGSUFFERING

The fruit of the Spirit is love, joy, peace, longsuffering.

—GALATIANS 5:22

To be longsuffering means to be patient. When we are patient, we trust God and love others, even when things don't go our way. Just think how patient Jesus is with us. When we sin, He forgives us because He loves us. Even when we say we're sorry and then sin again, He keeps forgiving us.

Jesus lives inside those of us who love Him. This means we can be patient and understanding too, even when other people say or do things that hurt us.

Question: What does it mean to be longsuffering?

Answer: To be longsuffering means to be patient.

Who are some people with whom you need to be patient?

Thank You, Lord Jesus, for the strength to be patient with others. Thank You so much for being patient with me. Amen.

GOD'S SPIRIT
BRINGS KINDNESS

The fruit of the Spirit is love, joy, peace, longsuffering, kindness.

—GALATIANS 5:22

Jesus was always kind to people who were hurting. He cared how they felt and wanted them to be happy and well. Since we want to be like Jesus, we will care how others feel too. The Holy Spirit will help us to be kind by saying and doing what will makes others glad.

The Bible says, "Be kind to one another, tenderhearted, forgiving one another, even as God for Christ's sake has forgiven you" (Eph. 4:32).

Question: How can you show kindness?

Answer: I can show kindness by saying and doing what will make others glad.

Let's Talk About It

Name someone who needs to be shown kindness today. How can you show this person kindness?

Let's Pray Together

Thank You, Jesus, for always being so kind to me. And thank You for helping me to be kind to others. Amen.

God's Spirit Brings Goodness

The fruit of the Spirit is love, joy, peace, longsuffering, kindness, goodness.

—Galatians 5:22

Jesus is the only person who ever lived who was always truly good. But now Jesus' Spirit lives inside of us, so *His* goodness can be lived out through *us*!

To be good means that we think, say, and do what pleases God. God's Spirit works in us to produce goodness. The Bible says that those who trust Jesus as their Savior are "created in Christ Jesus for good works" (Eph. 2:10).

Question: What is goodness?

Answer: Goodness is thinking, saying, and doing what pleases God.

Let's Talk About It

Who is the only person who ever lived who was always good? Does He now live inside of you? Then His goodness is inside you, isn't it? Let's ask Jesus to let His goodness show through us.

Let's Pray Together

Lord Jesus, I'm so thankful You live inside of me since I've invited You into my life. I want You to live Your life through mine. Thank You for the Holy Spirit, who works to make me like You. Amen.*

---

* If the child has not yet prayed to receive Christ as Lord and Savior, you may want to read again the session entitled "Jesus Is Lord and Savior" on page 60. Or you may want to alter the prayer to better fit the child's situation.

81

God's Spirit Brings Faithfulness

The fruit of the Spirit is love, joy, peace, longsuffering, kindness, goodness, faithfulness.

—Galatians 5:22

Let's Listen

The Bible speaks many times about the need for Christians to be faithful. When someone is faithful, he can be trusted. When a person is faithful, he can be depended on. A faithful person can be counted on to do what he says he will do.

We should first be faithful to God. We show Him our faithfulness by how we live every day. If we learn to read the Bible and obey it, if we pray, if we tell others about Jesus, and if we go to church whenever we can, we are showing faithfulness to God.

We should also be faithful to those around us. We should always be loyal to our family and friends and never say anything unkind about them. When we tell someone we will do something for them, we should do it! This will show that we can be trusted and that we are faithful.

Let's Answer

Question: How can you know if a person is faithful?

Answer: When a person is faithful, he can be trusted to do what he says he will do.

Let's Talk About It

The Bible says that God can be trusted to keep His promises. (Read 1 Thessalonians 5:24 and 1 John 1:9.) If we can trust God to keep His promises, shouldn't others be able to trust us, as God's children, to keep our promises? What are some ways that you can show faithfulness?

Let's Pray Together

Dear God, make me a faithful person by Your Holy Spirit. I want You and other people to know I can be depended on to do those things I promise to do. Amen.

GOD'S SPIRIT BRINGS GENTLENESS

The fruit of the Spirit is love, joy, peace, longsuffering, kindness, goodness, faithfulness, gentleness.
—GALATIANS 5:22–23

Let's Listen

People can sometimes be cruel. They can shout bad things that hurt others. They can be unkind and hateful in the way they act. Often people act meanly because they have been treated meanly. Most of those who try to hurt others have been hurt in some way themselves.

So when people are mean to us, we should not be mean to them. Instead, we should be gentle and try to understand that they probably are hurting inside. We should always remember the Golden Rule that Jesus gave us: "Whatever you want men to do to you, you also do to them" (Matt. 7:12).

That's the best way to live!

Question: What is the Golden Rule?

Answer: "Whatever you want men to do to you, you also do to them" (Matt. 7:12).

Let's Talk About It

Can you think of someone who has not been nice to you? How should you act toward that person?

Let's Pray Together

Dear God, help me to always remember the Golden Rule and to live by what it says. Make me truly gentle with all people. Amen.

God's Spirit Brings
Self-Control

The fruit of the Spirit is love, joy, peace, longsuffering, kindness, goodness, faithfulness, gentleness, and self-control.

—Galatians 5:22–23

Self-control means we are able to control how we act. If a person is self-controlled, he doesn't pout or throw temper tantrums. He doesn't eat too much food. He isn't controlled by bad habits.

When Jesus is Lord of every part of our lives, we have self-control. The person who is self-controlled is learning to do what is right even when he doesn't feel like it. What he wants doesn't control him. God controls him.

We have been learning about the fruit that the Holy Spirit makes to grow in our lives. Some people call the different parts of this fruit *Christian virtues*. That just means that the Holy Spirit helps us live more and more like Jesus, as we let Him control our lives.

Let's Answer

Question: What is self-control?

Answer: Self-control means that I am able to control how I act.

Question: How can you have self-control?

Answer: I can have self-control by letting Jesus be the Lord of every part of my life.

Question: Who makes Christian virtues grow in you?

Answer: The Holy Spirit makes Christian virtues grow in me.

Let's Talk About It

What are some times when it's hard to control how you act? If you have asked Jesus into your life, you can do what is right at those times, even when you don't feel like it. Ask Jesus to help you.

Lord Jesus, You know the times when I need self-control. I'm asking You now to be Lord in those times. Thank You that Your Spirit makes self-control grow in those people who love You. Amen.

V

HOW TO MAKE GOD HAPPY

FAITH IN GOD

Without faith it is impossible to please [God].
—HEBREWS 11:16

We become Christians by faith in Jesus Christ. To have faith means to believe in something we can't see, touch, or hear and to know without a doubt that what we believe is true. Faith is a gift we can ask God to give us.

Christians show God that they have faith in Him by believing and doing what He says in His Word, the Bible. This pleases God. God is also pleased when we trust Him to take care of us. He knows what is best for us.

You can show you have faith in God by praying to Him, telling your friends about Jesus, obeying your parents, and doing whatever you know will please your Father in heaven.

Question: What does it mean to have faith in God?

Answer: To have faith in God means to believe in Him even though I can't see Him. I show faith in God when I believe what He says in His Word, the Bible.

There is one thing that we *must* have to please God. What is it?

Thank You, Lord Jesus, for the gift of faith in You. Please give me faith to believe in You always and to trust You to take care of me in the best way. Amen.

God Has a Family

> But as many as received Him, to them He gave the
> right to become children of God, even to those who
> believe in His name.
>
> —John 1:12

Let's Listen

You have two families! You belong to the family you live with, but you also belong to the family of God if you have asked Jesus to be your Savior. God's family is made up of all those who have invited Jesus into their lives. The Bible says that God gave those people the right to become His children. Everyone who has received Jesus as Lord and Savior is a child of God.

God knows it is very hard to live without a family. That's why He has given us a big family called the church. When you gather with other Christians, they are more than just your friends. They are also your brothers and sisters in Christ. We meet together each Sunday as a church to worship God.

Other Christians can help you live for Jesus, and you can help them do the same. That's why it's important to be with other Christians. When Christians get together to talk about how wonderful Jesus is, the Bible calls this *fellowship*.

Let's Answer

Question: Why should you be with other Christians?

Answer: Because Christians can help each other live for Jesus.

Let's Talk About It

Name some things we do at church that help us grow as Christians.

Let's Pray Together

Dear God, I'm glad to be part of Your wonderful family. Thank You for the chance to meet together with other Christians to worship You and to learn how we can serve You better. Amen.

You Can Talk to God

> Whatever you ask in My name, that I will do, that the Father may be glorified in the Son.
>
> —John 14:13

Prayer is talking to God. We can talk to Him about anything. He loves for us to come to Him with all of our needs, joys, secrets, and dreams. He is always ready to listen.

We are to pray in Jesus' name. This means we can ask for things from God as though Jesus Himself were asking, so we must always remember to ask for things that would please Jesus. When He answers our prayers we see His power at work.

Let's Answer

Question: What is prayer?

Answer: Prayer is talking to God.

Question: In whose name are you to pray?

Answer: I am to pray in the name of Jesus.

Let's Talk About It

Look again at the wonderful promise Jesus made in John 14:13. What is something that will please God that hasn't happened yet? Ask God to make it happen in Jesus' name.

Let's Pray Together

Dear God, I'm asking You now to [place your request here]. I know that when You answer this request it will bring glory to You. I ask You to answer my prayer because I am praying in Jesus' name. Amen.

95

God Wrote You a Love Letter

All Scripture is given by inspiration of God.
— 2 Timothy 3:16

God has written you a love letter! God's love letter to you is the Bible. In the Bible, we find out how very much God loves us, even to the point of sending Jesus to die for us. The Bible tells us what God is like and how we can know Him.

The Bible is God's Word and God cannot lie. (Read Titus 1:2 and Hebrews 6:18.) Through its history, the church has believed the Bible is true. Though some people have tried to prove there are mistakes in the Bible, they have never found even one! Because God loves us, He has given us a book we can trust. It is His love letter to His children.

Question: What does the Bible tell us?

Answer: The Bible tells us what God is like, how we can know Him and how we can live for Him.

Have you ever received a card in the mail or an email? Were you excited to hear what it said? God has sent you a letter called the Bible. He wants you to listen carefully to what He wrote to you.

Thank You, God, for Your holy Word, the Bible. Teach me to respect, love, and obey Your Word. In Jesus' name. Amen.

You Can Tell Others

Follow Me, and I will make you fishers of men.
—Matthew 4:19

If we know Jesus, we will want others to know Him too. The good news about Him is too wonderful to keep to ourselves. When we tell others about Jesus, we feel a special joy inside. What could be more exciting than bringing someone else to Jesus so they can know Him too! Jesus says that if we follow Him, we will learn how to "fish for men," which is the same thing as telling others about Jesus.

The Bible says, "For I am not ashamed of the gospel of Christ, for it is the power of God to salvation for everyone who believes" (Rom. 1:16).

We should never be ashamed of the good news about Jesus. It's the best news the world will ever hear! How happy it makes us to tell others about Jesus!

Question: If you follow Jesus, what will you become?

Answer: I will become a "fisher of men" (Matt. 4:19).

Who are some people you know who need to hear the good news about Jesus? When will you tell them about Him?

Thank You, Jesus, for letting me tell others about You. I'm glad that I can tell people the best news they will ever hear. Help me never to be afraid to talk to my friends about You. In Jesus' name, amen.

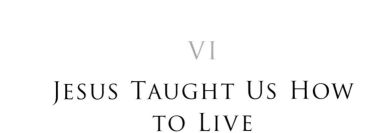

VI

Jesus Taught Us How to Live

BLESSED ARE THE POOR
IN SPIRIT

Blessed are the poor in spirit, For theirs is the kingdom of heaven.

—MATTHEW 5:3

One day Jesus taught a lot of people who gathered around Him on a mountainside. We call the message He gave the Sermon on the Mount. In that sermon, Jesus told the people how to live so they would please God and be blessed.

When Jesus said we would be blessed if we followed His teachings, He meant we would be happy if we followed them. He said first: "Blessed [or happy] are the poor in spirit, for theirs is the kingdom of heaven" (Matt. 5:3). This means those people who realize they are not good enough to come to God on their own are happy. Why? Because they are the only ones able to trust Jesus to bring them to God. They will live in the kingdom of heaven.

Question: Is anyone good enough to get to heaven on his own?

Answer: No. We must trust in Jesus to bring us to God and to heaven.

Some people think they're good enough to come to God without believing in Jesus. We call this "spiritual pride," which is sort of like bragging or thinking we're better than we really are. Jesus taught us to be "poor in spirit," to realize that we must have His goodness in us. Have you come to God as one who is "poor in spirit"?

Dear God, I know I'm not good enough to come live with You in heaven. But I'm glad You will accept me anyway because I have received Jesus, Your Son. Help me always to know my need for You so I can be happy and receive Your true riches. In Jesus' name, amen.

Blessed Are Those
Who Mourn

Let's Remember

> Blessed are those who mourn, For they shall be comforted.
>
> —Matthew 5:4

Let's Listen

Think of this! Jesus said that people who are sad can be blessed and happy. It can be a good thing to be sad if we are sad about the things that make God sad. A man once prayed, "Let my heart be broken by the things that break the heart of God."* Many of those who are sad now will rejoice in the future.

Sad things happen in every person's life. When we are sad, we can feel that Jesus is very close to us. That's why Jesus said, "Blessed are those who mourn, For they shall be comforted."

---

* The late Dr. Bob Pierce, founder of World Vision and Samaritan's Purse.

Question: When is a special time that we can feel Jesus is very close to us?

Answer: We can feel Jesus is very close to us when we are sad.

Let's Talk About It

Do you remember a very sad time in your life? Remember that Jesus wants to comfort you and be very close to you in times like that.

Let's Pray Together

> Thank You, Lord Jesus, that You don't leave Your children sad forever. You turn their sadness into joy. Sorrow is turned into joy before You.** Amen.

** Job 41:22

BLESSED ARE THE GENTLE

Blessed are the meek, For they shall inherit the earth.

—MATTHEW 5:5

We've already learned that when we are gentle we will obey the Golden Rule. That rule says, "Whatever you want men to do to you, you also do to them" (Matt. 7:12).

Some people don't think it's smart to be gentle and to obey the Golden Rule. They think you should fight for everything and be mean if you need to be. That is how to get what you want, they say.

But we know better! Jesus promised that those who are gentle will one day inherit the Earth. That's a present worth waiting for!

Question: What will happen one day to those who are gentle?

Answer: They will inherit the Earth.

What does the Golden Rule say? What were some times when you obeyed this rule?

Thank You, Lord, for the wonderful future I have with You! Teach me to be gentle so that I may inherit the earth. In Jesus' name, amen.

BLESSED ARE THOSE WHO HUNGER AND THIRST FOR RIGHTEOUSNESS

Let's Remember

> Blessed are those who hunger and thirst for righteousness, For they shall be filled.
>
> —MATTHEW 5:6

Let's Listen

When we're hungry, we want food. When we're thirsty, we want water. All people desire food and water from time to time. We should want to please God just as much as a hungry boy wants food or a thirsty girl wants water. That's what it means to hunger and thirst after righteousness. We can ask God to give us that desire. If you have that desire, it means you want to please God in all that you think, say, and do.

When we are filled with the Holy Spirit, we have God's power to live the kind of life that pleases God.

Question: What does it mean to hunger and thirst for righteousness?

Answer: It means to desire to please God in all that I think, say, and do.

Do you want to please God in everything you think, say, and do? What are some ways you can please God?

Dear God, I want to please You with all of my heart. Fill me with Your Holy Spirit so I will have power to be pleasing to You. In Jesus' name, amen.

Blessed Are the Merciful

Blessed are the merciful, For they shall obtain mercy.

—Matthew 5:7

"He ought to be punished!"

Have you ever heard anyone say that? Maybe a boy or girl did something really bad and deserves to be punished, but how beautiful it is when we are kind and show mercy to that child. To show mercy means not punishing someone who really deserves it and instead choosing to forgive that person from our heart.

We should never forget that we deserve to be punished too. We should be punished for our sins. But Jesus had mercy on us and took the punishment Himself! Just think how much He loves us.

Since Jesus showed mercy to us, we should show mercy to others. If we show mercy to others now, we will receive mercy later.

Let's Answer

Question: What is the reward for showing mercy to others?

Answer: God will show mercy to me.

Let's Talk About It

Who can you show mercy to right now?

Let's Pray Together

> Lord Jesus, You have been so merciful to me. You have forgiven all my sins and taken all my punishment. Help me now to be merciful to others. I ask this in Your name. Amen.

BLESSED ARE THE PURE IN HEART

> Blessed are the pure in heart, For they shall see God.
>
> —MATTHEW 5:8

When Jesus comes into your life, He makes your heart—that secret part of you that only God can see—clean and pure. If Jesus is in your life, you will one day see God the Father.

The prophet Jeremiah said, "The heart is deceitful above all things, and desperately wicked; who can know it?" (Jer. 17:9). Our hearts can try to play tricks on us. Sometimes we think it is better to do what is wrong than to do what God says. Evil ways and evil thoughts are natural when a person doesn't know Jesus. The person without Jesus may think and do things even he doesn't understand. And even those who love Jesus may sometimes do and think wrong things. But they can and will change because Jesus lives in them.

After King David had sinned he prayed, "Create in me a clean heart, O God, and renew a steadfast spirit within me" (Ps. 51:10). God can give you a pure heart.

Let's Answer

Question: Who can make your heart clean and pure?

Answer: Jesus can make my heart clean and pure.

Let's Talk About It

Why does your heart need to be made clean and pure by Jesus? What does the Bible mean when it says our hearts are deceitful and wicked?

Let's Pray Together

Dear God, my prayer is the same as King David's prayer of long ago. "Create in me a clean heart, O God, and renew a steadfast spirit within me." In Jesus' name, amen.

BLESSED ARE THE
PEACEMAKERS

Let's Remember

Blessed are the peacemakers, For they shall be called sons of God.

—MATTHEW 5:9

Let's Listen

A peacemaker is someone who tries to turn enemies into friends. It is not always an easy job. Sometimes people who are angry at each other will become angry at a peacemaker too. This is what happened to Jesus, the Prince of Peace.

Our Bible verse promises that peacemakers will be called sons of God. Children of God are those who have Jesus living inside of them. Jesus brings peace and happiness into our lives. As children of God we want others to know this peace and happiness too. God has given us a special job of bringing peace between people who don't like each other. That's our job: turning enemies into friends!

Question: What is the reward given to peacemakers?

Answer: Peacemakers will be called sons of God.

Let's Talk About It

Can you think of anyone you know who is angry with someone else? What can you do to help them be friends?

Let's Pray Together

Dear God, help people to know that I belong to You because I work to turn enemies into friends. In Jesus' name, amen.

115

BLESSED ARE THOSE WHO ARE PERSECUTED FOR RIGHTEOUSNESS' SAKE

> Blessed are those who are persecuted for righteousness' sake, For theirs is the kingdom of heaven.
>
> —MATTHEW 5:10

There are times when Christians are called to suffer for the name of Jesus. Peter, one of Jesus' disciples, said, "For to this you were called, because Christ also suffered for us, leaving us an example, that you should follow His steps" (1 Pet. 2:21). It is a very high honor to suffer for Christ and the gospel. Some Christians lose friends when they follow Jesus. Some Christians are laughed at. Others are cursed. Some are even killed because they stand up for Jesus.

You will be called upon to suffer for Jesus in some way some day. Then you will know what it means to be "persecuted for righteousness' sake." You never need to be afraid of this. Those who suffer for Jesus know that He is with them. And just think of the reward! "For theirs is the kingdom of heaven."

Let's Answer

Question: What is the reward for those who are persecuted for righteousness' sake?

Answer: Theirs is the kingdom of heaven.

Let's Talk About It

Why should we never be afraid to suffer for Jesus? How can we be prepared to suffer for Jesus?

Let's Pray Together

Dear God, I know it is an honor to suffer for You and Your cause. Help me never to be afraid to live for You, whatever the cost. Help me never to be ashamed of You. I love You, Lord. Keep me true to You all the days of my life. In Jesus' name, amen.

VII.
SOME VERY
IMPORTANT WORDS

REPENTANCE

Repent and believe the gospel.

—MARK 1:15

Sin is anything in our life that does not please God. Sin is not caring about what God wants and living just to please ourselves. When a person repents, he stops living for himself and starts living for God. He changes his mind about the way he should live.

Before we can really live as God desires, we must repent. That means we must stop living just to please ourselves. When we repent, we turn around and go God's way. Then we will want to think and do only what will make God happy.

Question: What happens when you repent?

Answer: When I repent, I stop living just to please myself and start living to please God. I turn from any bad things I am doing and I go God's way.

What are some thoughts or actions from which you should turn away?

> *Dear God, I turn from anything in my life that doesn't please You. I turn to You and ask You to help me live in a way that pleases You. I want to go Your way. In Jesus' name, amen.*

SALVATION

> For whoever calls upon the name of the Lord will
> be saved.
>
> —ROMANS 10:13

Our greatest need is for salvation. When someone asks God to forgive him for his sins and receives Jesus into his life, that person is saved.

First, he is saved from being punished for his sins. Punishment for sins would have put us in a place far from God forever after we die. But we are saved from that penalty, thanks to Jesus. "For God so loved the world that He gave His only begotten Son, that whoever believes in Him should not perish but have everlasting life" (John 3:16).

A believer in Jesus is also saved from wasting his life. Now we can live lives that please God. If Jesus lives inside of us we want to please God.

Question: What are believers in Jesus saved from?

Answer: Believers in Jesus are saved from being punished for their sins. Jesus took the punishment for us.

Question: What are believers in Jesus able to do once they are saved?

Answer: Believers in Jesus can learn to live lives that please God because the Holy Spirit will help them.

Let's Talk About It

The word *salvation* means to be rescued out of some danger. What danger were we in before we invited Jesus into our lives?

Let's Pray Together

Thank You, Jesus, for taking the punishment for my sins when You died on the cross. Thank You that I can be saved from the penalty of my sins by trusting You to save me. Help me to live a life that makes You happy. In Jesus' name, amen.

REVERENCE

Let's Remember

> God is greatly to be feared in the assembly of the
> saints, And to be held in reverence by all those who
> are around Him.
>
> —PSALM 89:7

Let's Listen

To reverence God means to have great respect for His
power, His love, and His name. When the Bible tells
us to fear God, it means we are to give God the very
highest respect and honor as our heavenly Father. We
should *never* take His name lightly nor joke about Him.
He is God. He has the power to do anything. He can
create storms and He can stop them. He can create life
and He can take it. God created everything there is.

When we reverence God, we are amazed at His wonderful acts. We bow before Him in worship, love and
obedience.

Question: What does it mean to reverence God?

Answer: To reverence God means to have a great respect for His power, His love, and His name.

Let's Talk About It

What are some ways you can show reverence for God?

Let's Pray Together

Dear God, I bow in reverence before You. I praise You for Your power, Your love, and Your name. I love You and I respect You. In Jesus' name, amen.

OBEY

Let's Remember

Children, obey your parents in the Lord, for this is right.

—EPHESIANS 6:1

Let's Listen

God has placed some people in our lives that we are to obey. He has done this because He loves us. These people are given to protect us and help us. Our parents, teachers, pastors, and policemen are all gifts to us from God. We are to obey what they tell us, unless what they tell us would make us sin against God. When we obey, we do what we are told to do. When we do this for the Lord, we show Jesus that we want to obey His Word, the Bible. Jesus said, "If you love me, keep My commandments" (John 14:15). We should always obey what God says in His Word.

There is a special promise for those who obey their parents. The Bible says they will have a long, happy life. (Read Ephesians 6:1-3.)

Question: What does the Bible promise if you obey your parents?

Answer: I will have a long, happy life.

Name some people in your life you should obey. What is the one book you should always obey?

Dear Lord, I pray that I will obey those You have placed over me to protect and help me. May I always obey Your holy Word, the Bible. In Jesus' name, amen.

FORGIVE

> Be kind to one another, tenderhearted, forgiving one another, even as God in Christ forgave you.
>
> —EPHESIANS 4:32

What do you do when someone is mean to you? Do you become angry and look for a way to be mean to them? People who will not forgive others can become hateful. Hateful people are never fun to be around. Some people get sick because they won't forgive the person who hurt them. When we do not forgive others, we cannot become good friends with Jesus.

If you don't forgive when others treat you unfairly you will become angry. You won't have fun and you won't be fun to be around. And we're never happy when we aren't close to Jesus. When we try to please Him, then we are truly happy.

Jesus has forgiven us for all our sins. Since He has forgiven us, we should forgive others.

Let's Answer

Question: Why should you forgive others?

Answer: I should forgive others because Jesus has forgiven me.

Let's Talk About It

Is there someone who has hurt you whom you need to forgive?

Let's Pray Together

Thank You, God, for forgiving me of all my sins against You. Just as You have forgiven me for hurting You, I now forgive all those who have hurt me. Help me always to forgive quickly when I am wronged. In Jesus' name, amen.

LOVE

> By this all will know that you are My disciples, if you have love for one another.
>
> —John 13:35

People will know that we are Jesus' followers, His disciples, if we love one another. Everything about us should show love.

The apostle Paul told us what this love of God is like. "Love suffers long and is kind; love does not envy; love does not parade itself, is not puffed up; does not behave rudely, does not seek its own, is not provoked, thinks no evil; does not rejoice in iniquity, but rejoices in the truth; bears all things, believes all things, hopes all things, endures all things. Love never fails" (1 Cor. 13:4-8).

When people see that kind of love in us they will know we are Jesus' disciples!

Question: How will others know that you are following Jesus?

Answer: If I show love for others.

What are some ways you can show love to others? What first step should you take right now?

Dear God, help me to love others as You do. Then everyone will know I am a follower of Jesus. In His name, amen.

Disciple

If you continue in My word, then you are My disciples indeed.

—John 8:31

A disciple is someone who is following Jesus. A disciple is a learner. A follower of Jesus learns more about Him and His ways.

Here are some things you can do to learn more about Jesus and His ways. You can talk to God in prayer. Tell Him everything you think about. You can listen to God's Word, the Bible. As you learn to read the Bible, the world's most wonderful book, you can tell others the good news about Jesus. Then they can know Him too. You can worship God with other Christians at church. This is a time when we get to know others in God's big, wonderful family.

If you do these things, you will learn more about Jesus and His ways.

Let's Answer

Question: What does it mean to be a disciple of Jesus?

Answer: It means that I am following Jesus and learning more about Him and His ways.

Let's Talk About It

Name some things we can do to learn more about Jesus and His ways.

Let's Pray Together

Dear God, help me to be a good follower of Jesus. Help me to always be learning more about Him and His ways. In His name, amen.

CHRISTIAN

> And the disciples were first called Christians in Antioch.
>
> —Acts 11:26

A person is not a Christian just because he goes to church or is a church member. A person is not a Christian just because he has been baptized or christened. A person is not a Christian just because he does kind deeds. A Christian may do all of these things, but that is not what makes a person a Christian. A Christian is a person who has Jesus Christ living inside of him or her. If you can truly say that Jesus is Lord of your life and if you believe that Jesus rose from the dead, you are a Christian and Jesus lives in you. (Read Romans 10:9.)

Question: What is a Christian?

Answer: A Christian is someone who has Jesus Christ living inside of him.

When people look at your life, can they tell you are a Christian?

Lord Jesus, thank You for living inside of me. Teach me to live in such a way that people will know that I belong to You. In Your name, amen.

APPENDIX

What Christians Believe

Let's Remember

I believe in God, the Father almighty, creator of heaven and earth. I believe in Jesus Christ, God's only Son, our Lord, who was conceived by the Holy Spirit, born of the Virgin Mary, suffered under Pontius Pilate, was crucified, died, and was buried; He descended into hell. The third day He rose again; He ascended into heaven, and is seated at the right hand of the Father, from there He will come again to judge the living and the dead. I believe in the Holy Spirit, the holy catholic church, the communion of saints, the forgiveness of sins, the resurrection of the body, and the life everlasting. Amen.*

Let's Listen

When we recite a creed, we say what we believe and know is true. Long ago some Christians decided they should write down some of their most important beliefs. This

---

* Parents should help children understand words whose meanings may be difficult. For instance, *catholic* means "universal" and is a reference to the entire global church, not any particular denomination.

was done to help them stay away from wrong teachings that did not say the same things the Bible says.

What we have read is known as the Apostles' Creed. For many hundreds of years, Christians have been reciting this creed to remind them of some of their most important beliefs.

Today we are joined in faith with all those who have believed in Jesus throughout history. It is an honor to be part of that large group of people through the centuries who belong to Jesus. They are our brothers and sisters in Christ. Let's recite the Apostles' Creed again.

Let's Answer

Question: What is the Apostles' Creed?

Answer: The Apostles' Creed is a statement of some of the most important beliefs and truths of the Christian church.

Let's Talk About It

What are some words in this creed that you don't understand? Let's talk about what they mean.

Thank You, Father, that the truth about You and the truth about Your Son, the Lord Jesus, never changes. I'm glad my faith rests in beliefs that have always been true and always will be true. Amen.

Some Favorite Bible Stories

---

[*] Acts 6–7 gives the full story of Stephen for older children.

To Contact the Authors

www.globaladvance.org